MIDLAND PARK MEMORIAL LIBRARY, NJ
3 9142 09162295 6

Y0-GEM-097

Sayyidah Fatimah (A)
3

Heavenly Children

The Best Daughter

Midland Park Memorial Library
250 Godwin Ave
Midland Park, NJ 07432

Kisa Kids Publications

Dedication

This book is dedicated to the beloved Imām of our time (AJ). May Allāh (swt) hasten his reappearance and help us to become his true companions.

Acknowledgements

Prophet Muḥammad (s): The pen of a writer is mightier than the blood of a martyr.

True reward lies with Allāh, but we would like to sincerely thank the efforts of Shaykh Salim Yusufali, Brother Aliakbar Shaheidari, Sisters Sabika Mithani, Fatemah Mithani, Amna Hussain, Asieh Zarghami, Zahra Sabur, Sajeda Merchant, Kisae Nazar, Sarah Assaf, Nadia Dossani, Fathema Abidi, Fatemeh Eslami, Fatima Hussain, Fatemah Meghji, Sukaena Kalyan, and Zehra Abbas. We would especially like to thank Nainava Publications for their contributions. May Allāh bless them in this world and the next.

Preface

Prophet Muḥammad (s): Nurture and raise your children in the best way. Raise them with the love of the Prophets and the Ahlul Bayt (a).

Literature is an influential form of media that often shapes the thoughts and views of an entire generation. Therefore, in order to establish an Islāmic foundation for the future generations, there is a dire need for compelling Islamic literature. Over the past several years, this need has become increasingly prevalent throughout Islāmic centers and schools everywhere. Due to the growing dissonance between parents, children, society, and the teachings of Islām and the Ahlul Bayt (a), this need has become even more pressing. Al-Kisa Foundation, along with its subsidiary, Kisa Kids Publications, was conceived in an effort to help bridge this gap with the guidance of ʿulamah and the help of educators. We would like to make this a communal effort and platform. Therefore, we sincerely welcome constructive feedback and help in any capacity.

The goal of the *Heavenly Children* series is to foster the love of Ahlul Bayt (a) in children and to help them establish the 14 Maʿṣūmīn as their role models. We hope that you and your children enjoy these books and use them as a means to achieve this goal, inshāʾAllāh.

We pray to Allāh to give us the strength and *tawfīq* to perform our duties and responsibilities.

With Duʿās,
Nabi R. Mir (Abidi)

Disclaimer: Religious texts have ***not*** been translated verbatim so as to meet the developmental and comprehension needs of children.

Copyright © 2016; 2019 by Al-Kisa Foundation; SABA Global

All rights reserved. First edition 2016. Second edition 2019. No part of this publication may be reproduced, distributed, or transmitted in any form or by any means, including photocopying, recording, or other electronic or mechanical methods, without the prior written permission of the publisher, except in the case of brief quotations embodied in critical reviews and certain other noncommercial uses permitted by copyright law. For permission requests, please write to the publisher at the address below.

Kisa Kids Publications
4415 Fortran Court
San Jose, CA 95134
(260) KISA-KID [547-2543]

Ahmad's family was preparing for a big trip to visit the fourteen Ma'soomeen. Baba had just told him about the courage of Imam Ali (a), even as a child.

"Wow, that was an incredible story, Baba. InshaAllah, I can be brave like Imam Ali (a), and stop bullies when I see them!" Ahmad nodded with determination. "Who else will we be visiting on our trip?" he asked.

His mother replied, "While we are in Medina visiting the Prophet (s), we will also visit his daughter, Sayyidah Fatimah Zahra (a)! While we do not know the exact place of her grave, we know that she became a shaheedah* in Medina, and she is most likely buried somewhere there."

"I remember Sayyidah Fatimah (a) is known as the greatest lady. What was she like?" asked Ahmad.

"You're right, Sayyidah Fatimah (a) is the greatest woman of all time! She was also a great wife to Imam Ali (a)! And because she used to work very hard, Prophet Muhammad (s) gave her a very special gift."

"Was it a house?" guessed Ahmad.

Mama laughed heartily, "No, it wasn't a house! It was even more special than that. It was the tasbeeh of Sayyidah Fatimah (a) that we recite after salaah: 'Allahu Akbar' 34 times, 'Alhamdulillah' 33 times, and 'SubhaanAllah' 33 times. Salaah is like a flower, and this Tasbeeh is what gives the flower its beautiful aroma!"

"You always tell me how important it is to recite that Tasbeeh. It's definitely more special than a house!" Ahmad smiled. "Did Sayyidah Fatimah (a) have kids?" he asked.

"She had four children: Imam Hasan (a), Imam Husain (a), Sayyidah Zainab (a), and Sayyidah Umm Kulthoom (a)."

"Oh yeah! I know a little about them, and they were the greatest, too. She had to be the greatest mom!" exclaimed Ahmad.

"She sure was," said Mama. "In fact, Ahmad, not only was she a great mother to her children, but she was also like a mother to her father. Her own mother, Hadhrat Khadija, passed away when Sayyidah Fatimah (a) was very young. So, she would be the one to take care of the Noble Prophet (s) when the enemies would trouble him, and he respected her very much. In fact, he called her 'Umm Abiha' — the 'mother of her father' — because of how well she used to take care of him! Shall I tell you a story about how deeply she cared for her father?"

Ahmad nodded, sitting up intently, ready to listen.

*Shaheedah: someone who dies in the path of Allah

The hot afternoon sun beat down on the people of Medina as they worked tirelessly. Prophet Muhammad (s) had gotten news that the enemies of Islam were coming to attack the Muslims, and the whole city was in danger! After a discussion with his companions, the Prophet (s) decided that the best way to protect themselves was to dig a large trench around the city. All the men had been digging and digging for hours.

Everyone was hungry and thirsty, but there was no time to stop. All you could hear were the loud clunks of shovels and pickaxes hitting the dirt. Some people were picking up and piling rocks while others were scooping up the dirt, but nobody stopped working. The most beautiful sight was that of the Noble Prophet (s), working right alongside the men and guiding and encouraging them.

Everyone was on high alert, listening for the enemy's approach. The Muslims had been working very hard over the last few days to finish before the enemy arrived. After many more hours of digging, one of the men finally yelled out, "Tell the Prophet (s) we are done! We are finally done!"

The men rushed to the Prophet (s) and told him the good news. The Prophet (s) praised Allah for all His support. He then called out to all his Muslim followers to get ready, as the idol-worshipping Meccans could come at any time. All the soldiers headed home to eat, get dressed in battle clothes, and take up their weapons, ready to defend Islam.

The Prophet (s) walked to the edge of the trench and saw a large cloud of dust in the distance. The earth shook below his feet. The faint sound of horses' hooves could be heard in the distance. The enemy had arrived.

The Prophet (s) looked at his soldiers, who were dedicated, loyal, and strong. They were so tired, but full of hope and faith in Allah. As the enemy approached, they gathered their strength and prepared for a difficult war. The Prophet (s) himself was tired and had not eaten for three days, but he stood strong with a heart full of trust in Allah, determined to defend truth and justice.

He kept a steady eye on the arriving enemies. He had tried many times to make peace with them, but they insisted on fighting.

لا اله الا الله

Not too far in the distance, you could see the women of Medina coming out of their homes, scared and worried, but hopeful in Allah. They were praying to Allah for the Muslims to be successful against the attack of the enemies.

Meanwhile, one noble lady stood in her doorway, worried for everyone's well-being, but especially that of her father. This was Sayyidah Fatimah Zahra (a), the loyal and loving daughter of the Prophet (s). She knew how much effort and time he had invested the past few days in the service of Allah. She also knew that he had not had a meal in all that time.

Sayyidah Fatimah (a) loved her father very much, and it pained her to know how hungry he was. Even as a child, Sayyidah Fatimah (a) was known as "Umm Abiha," the "mother of her father," because of how she loved him dearly and cared for him.

As she thought about him in the battlefield, she couldn't help but wonder how tired and hungry he must be.

Just thinking about it moved her to action. She headed straight to the kitchen.

I'm going to cook the best possible food for my father! she thought to herself. However, all she could find in the house was some flour. What could she do with just flour?

Suddenly, a great idea came to her mind! She quickly lit a fire and warmed the tanoor*. She whispered a "Bismillah" before starting, then continued reciting dhikr, Allah's praise, as she began kneading the flour into dough. Working carefully, she shaped the dough into small circles. Then, she put the dough into the tanoor and watched it bake into bread.

*Tanoor: an open brick oven

When Sayyidah Fatimah (a) finished, she felt a little upset! She thought to herself, *is this really all I can give to my father?*

She swallowed hard and held back tears. However, remembering how hungry her father was, she thanked Allah for even this simple offering, quickly wrapped the fresh-baked bread in a red cloth, and headed towards the battlefield.

As Sayyidah Fatimah (a) walked, the thought of her hungry father kept pushing her to move more quickly. The blistering sun of Medina beat down on her face, and she could hear the clamoring of soldiers in battle.

She continued onward. She saw that some of the enemies had managed to cut across the trench and were already in combat with the Muslim army.

When the Prophet (s) caught sight of Sayyidah Fatimah (a), he quickly dismounted his horse and hurried towards her.

The Prophet (s) leaned down with kindness and tenderness in his eyes and greeted her with salaam. Sayyidah Fatimah (a) happily uncovered the bread, which was still warm, and presented it to her father.

He smiled. "Where did you get this from?" he asked.

Sayyidah Fatimah (a) answered warmly, "I baked them for you, dearest Father."

The Prophet (s) took a whiff of the fresh bread, gingerly broke off a piece, and took a bite. His face lit up with delight. "My dear Fatimah, this is the most delicious bread I have ever tasted!" he said. "Your bread is the first bite of food that I have had in three days!"

Sayyidah Fatimah (a) smiled from ear to ear. She was so grateful to be able to help him in this way. Affectionately, she kissed her father's hand. Now that the bread had been delivered, it was time for Sayyidah Fatimah (a) to leave the battlefield. Father and daughter bid each other farewell.

The Prophet (s) mounted his horse and rode back into the battlefield. As she watched him leave, Sayyidah Fatimah (a) couldn't help but notice that he looked taller, stronger, and more vibrant than the burning Medina sun.

Dhakhāʾir al-ʿUqbā, P. 47